Grammaropolis
PRESENTS

Nelson the Noun

Written by Coert Voorhees
Illustrations by Powerhouse Animation

Meet the Parts of Speech

I name a specific person, place, thing, or idea. It's a big responsibility, naming things— a responsibility that requires a certain attention to detail.

Nelson the Noun

Some people say I'm all over the place. Some people call me a ball of energy. I take that as a compliment, because I just like to go, go, go!

Vinny the Action Verb

I take the place of one or more Nouns or Pronouns. I always want the Noun's job, and I hang out with the Verb and Adjective.

Roger the Pronoun

I'm perfectly happy to link Nouns and Pronouns with the appropriate Adjectives, but it's not like I'm going to expend a lot of energy doing so.

Lucy the Linking Verb

I modify a Noun or Pronoun. I tell what kind, which one, how many, or how much. I pride myself on being the most artistic of the parts of speech.

Jake the Adjective

Gather 'round everybody and let's have ourselves a wonderful time. I just love bringing words and groups of words together, don't you?

Connie the Conjunction

I modify a Verb, Adjective, or other Adverb. I tell how, when, where, to what extent, and under what condition. I often end in –ly, but I don't have to.

Benny the Adverb

I express emotion!! Yep, I'm always here, always ready with my commas and exclamation points, just in case.

Izzy the Interjection

They call me Preposition because I'm pre-positioned. I'm first. At the front. Before every other word in the phrase? Got it?

Li'l Pete the Preposition

I am a chameleon. A spy. An undercover operative. I infiltrate the sentence and act as whatever part of speech suits me.

Slang

NELSON THE NOUN

© 2019 Grammaropolis

Graphic Design by Mckee Frazior
Printed by Friesens, Altona, Manitoba, Canada

Text and Illustrations © 2011 by Grammaropolis LLC

This book is typeset in Komika Text

Distributed throughout the world
by Ingram Publisher Services
www.ingrambook.com

Printed in Canada

Before Nelson opened up his own place, he worked at the Noun Office.

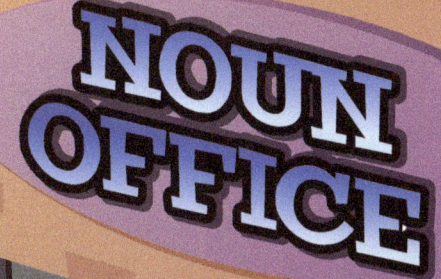

His job was to name people, places, things, and ideas.

1

He worked hard because he knew that Roger the pronoun always wanted to take his place.

Are you sure I can't help out?

2

Person

Lucy

Jake

policeman

Place

ALBUQUERQUE

WHAT FUN!

Antarctica!

PARIS

Thing

bubble

zipper

aardvark

snorkel

Organization was extremely important to Nelson.

Collective Noun Day was when Nelson used a singular noun to name a group. It was his least favorite day by far.

He packed light, only taking some of his favorite abstract nouns with him.

Nelson arrived at a desert island. He quickly named some of the nouns he saw, just to get it over with.

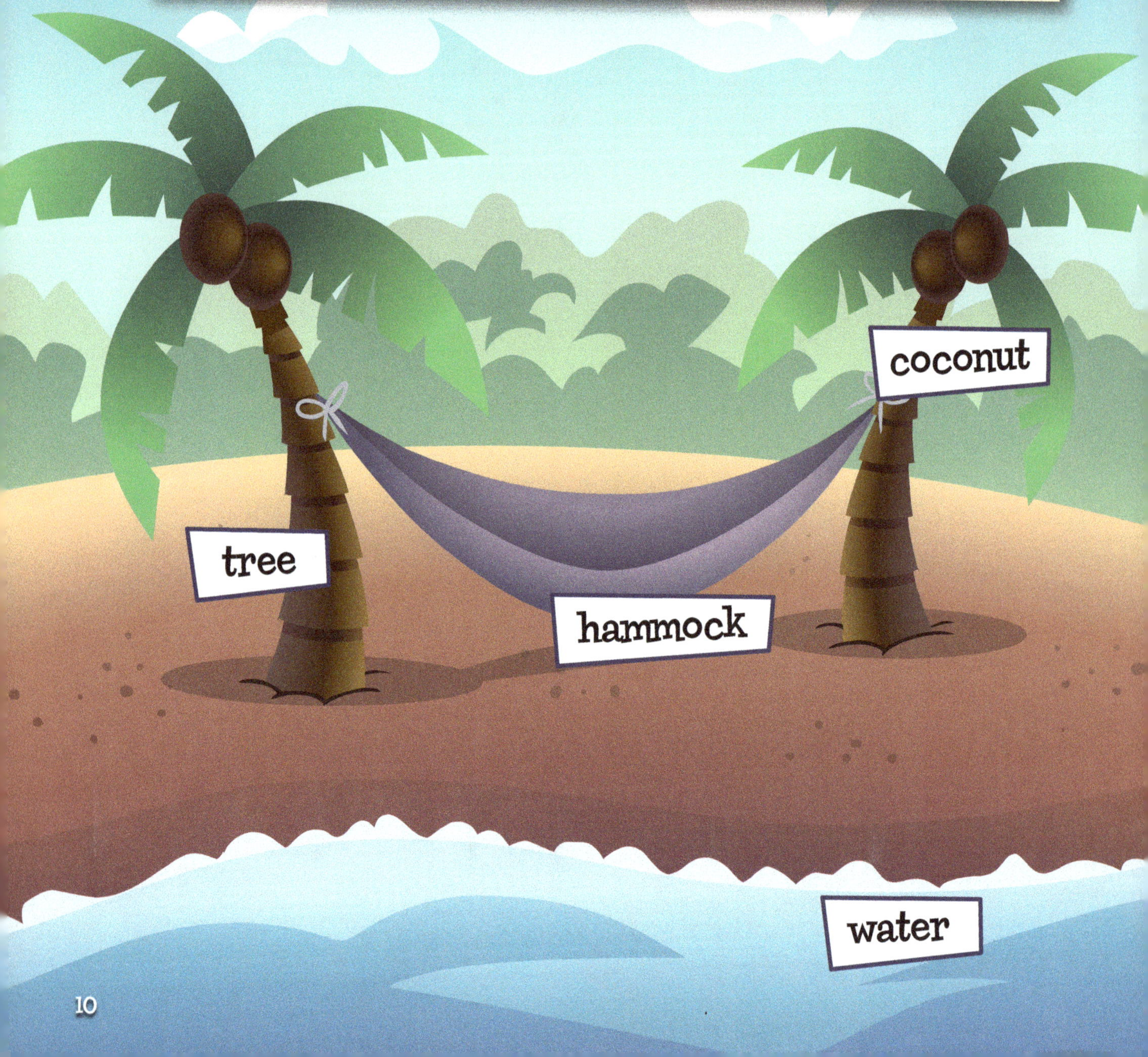

coconut

tree

hammock

water

volcano

beach

sand

After that, he settled in for a well-earned rest.

At first, Nelson loved his time away.

PEACE CONTENTMENT

After a while, however, he started to miss his friends. Without Vinny the action verb, he couldn't do anything.

He missed the other nouns and pronouns, and he missed Connie the conjunction, too.

Without Jake the adjective, he couldn't describe the sunset.

15

He tried to console himself with the abstract nouns he'd packed, but "courage" and "happiness" were nowhere to be found.
How did *this* get in here?
BOREDOM

He didn't even have Izzy the interjection to help him express his dismay.

Alas!

Oh, no.

Leaving Grammaropolis had been a terrible idea, so Nelson packed up and headed for home.

17

He discovered that things had not gone well without him.

Nelson got right to work. He started with the compound nouns: words stuck together to make a single noun.

Compound Nouns

eggplant

windshield

toothpaste

jack-in-the-box

seafood

grasshopper

Nelson had the office back to normal in no time.
Common Noun
Proper Noun
Cleveland
city
When in the course
document
Declaration of Independence
You look happy.
Maybe I just needed some time off.
neighbor
Reginald
We could use a little help out here!

22

Nelson's Noun Notes

PERSON

Ava is the most thoughtful girl in our entire school.

PLACE

Zak ate his lunch at a park in Chicago.

THING

There is a small stack of pennies on my dresser.

IDEA

We should all fight for fairness and equality.

A noun names a person, place, thing, or idea.

COMMON NOUNS

A common noun names a general person, place, thing, or idea.

When I was in the restaurant, I asked a lady what she knew about volcanoes.

EXAMPLES

restaurant
lady
volcanoes

PROPER NOUNS

A proper noun names a specific person, place, thing, or idea.

When I was in Burger King, I asked Lucy what she knew about Krakatoa and Vesuvius.

EXAMPLES

Burger King
Lucy
Krakatoa
Vesuvius

CONCRETE NOUNS

A **concrete noun** names a person, place, or thing that can be perceived by one or more of the five senses.

The **receptionist** yelled at me when I brought my **platypus** into the **museum**.

EXAMPLES

receptionist
platypus
museum

ABSTRACT NOUNS

An **abstract noun** is an idea or quality that can not be perceived by any of the five senses.

It is always best to live with **honor** and **courage** in your heart.

EXAMPLES

honor
courage

COMPOUND NOUNS

An compound noun is two or more words combined to make a single noun that names a person, place, thing, or idea. It can be one single word, two words, or words connected by hyphens.

My mother-in-law took me to the swimming pool after a dessert of strawberry shortcakes.

KNUCKLE HEAD

EXAMPLES
One word: shortcake
Two words: swimming pool
Hyphenated: mother-in-law

COLLECTIVE NOUNS

An collective noun is a singular noun that names a group.

Our band went to the zoo to see the school of fish, but an armory of aardvarks had escaped, so they closed the zoo and called in a squad of police.

EXAMPLES

school of fish
armory of aardvarks
squad of police

CPSIA information can be obtained
at www.ICGtesting.com
Printed in the USA
BVHW020504110519
547997BV00002B/6/P

9 781644 420157